DRAG ME THROUGH THE MESS

Jessica Mehta

For Chintan.

CONTENTS

DRAG ME THROUGH THE MESS

THE FIRST BLACK CLEOPATRA

This is naked: to stand

on famous stages, boards buffed soft
 by white feet in stark
contrast to your amber.
To know you're not

Cleopatra, but
the first Black Cleopatra. Who cares
about decades of training,
the scars and the hurts? Do this:

remove your wig before throngs
of pale schoolchildren wriggling
 in seats. Display your shorn locks,
a caged lion in the ring. Brush off
the shame, pretend it's a lover
who beckons with satin pillowcases
and says you're beautiful

with your hair wrapped, all
that natural kink. Strip off
your robe, showcase your body—
stand tall in your nakedness. Let
the spotlights warm your skin.

Hike up your lips, show us
your teeth. Bred good and strong
as a horse. What's the difference

between this and ancestors
on the auction block? We pay, we prod
we judge, we weigh. Afterward,

playbills rolled in damp hands,
rushings to taxis. And we'll say

She did good, real good,
that first black Cleopatra.

THE FALSITY OF FAST DEATHS

You picture broken necks quick
as wishing bones. I didn't know

the head could hang for hours, limp
and heavy as forgotten, un-squeezed
washcloths. That you still had to rush

them to the vet, cradle their little heads
like over-ripe persimmons. Cruel,

how the nearly dead are sentenced
to stare down the earth, the descent so slow—

welcoming black soil readying her grip
for the space spooned just for you.

SUMMER IN LORRAINE

Hot air balloons can only crash—
it took me fifteen years and five thousand
miles to watch nylon
candies *en flambé*
fall like parade castoffs
from the sky. In open fields, hands
sticky with crepe drippings, the lot of us
craned our necks and clutched our phones
with hungry impatience
for the cascade of exquisite collisions.

FINGERS IN THE FOXGLOVE

Dead, winged beasts fell
all around me—for a week
I stepped over a sparrow
chick fallen from the heavens
of my cottage. *He just gave up*
before giving life a chance. I asked you

if swans fly. You told me
you didn't know, but they're protected
by the monarchy. I walked on butterflies
at the garden and clawed
my fingers into the foxglove
soil. Here, I was to bury
the chick. When I picked him up,
he was hollow, eaten clean through,
a shell

of what he'd never become.

A CONSENTING PLATYPUS

The septuagenarian served me tea
in the garden of her thatched roof
cottage. Between spoons
of fish pie and too much Prosecco,
I told her about the best-selling erotica
I ghost write. How people don't like sex
until at least chapter nineteen.
She asked me about bestiality, which of us
animals are the nastiest. No, incest
and animals are my hard lines.
That's too bad, she demurred. *It's incredible
what one can do
with a consenting platypus.*

WHILE ZOZOBRA BURNS

My first night in Santa Fe I walked
for hours, lost in adobe mazes.
Parking lots were punctuated with hatch
green chilies tumbling in iron cages
while dusty sedans stood guard. Indigenous
red suns rested on fields of yellow
and for once a Native man told me I
was beautiful. *Say something
about her hips*, his friend with accent
thick as panocha whispered. *Esas caderas*—

but you shook those oiled braids
like whipsnakes and we matched
smiles over mesa cheekbones. Ashes
from the burned stick man built
nests in our plaits and I licked
charred woes from strangers
off my sun-cracked lips
as the big white cross guided me home.

SYMPTOMS OF AN END

Let me take you back to the Red Woods
where we drank cup after cup
of hazelnut coffee, sucked
the flesh from fish bones
and salty oysters from their homes.
I'd drive you again
over the state line,
my hand on your thick thigh
while the Oregon pines shake
with uncertainty
as if they don't realize
how incredible they are,
and you ask your empty hands,
Aren't these trees big enough?

THE WEIGHT OF SECRETS

Secrets weigh a tremendous lot,
you have to bear the brunt.
Make sure they're worth it—like a child
who cries something so fierce
you rock them to quiet, something
like complacency. Heavy burdens
only strengthen tendons, grow
muscles, densify bones so long
before the joints give out. I've carried

so many pinky swears they've built colonies
on my back. A dowager's hump
of things I'll never tell, words packed
with a blistering power my tongue
would burn before those syllables
can trickle fire down my chin.

RESURRECTION

I never wanted to come back,
not here, where the mess sloshed over
like cocktails staining pretty satined feet.
I came back for you, happy
to leave the palm trees behind,
the howler monkeys on the tin roof.
Oregon is where it began, and the Great
Northwest demanded the act end here, too.
(That's always where the hook kicks in)
Moving on,
we'll leave the rain behind, the gummy
bars tired from our twenties, the restaurants plundered
and the rain-pregnant streets already forgetting
our stampeding feet. I came back
to check for a pulse, see if We could be
pulled back sharp
from the edge of extinction.
How glorious that our vitality is so strong,
alive and kicking wildly, strong

like something shot at close range
yet demanding stubbornly to live.

GOD, MOTHER

The same aunt my mother hated,
she gifted me to her in the will. Like money
would fix me. And yet,

when my father died and my mother went crazy,
it wasn't my aunt's home sprawling
like a sea monster that swaddled me.
It was the black night with struggling
snow fall. The lurching twists
of the Oregon backroads. The wide
reaching arms of Forward, gas station
showers and stolen, pawned goods. I never saw
my aunt again. But I remember

her Mercedes that smelled of cigarettes
not like my father's. Her beautiful grown
children in their big houses. And how she looked
at us with pity, and a pinch
of disgust that wrinkled her perfect

face, the only crack in a façade she crafted
lovingly day after day after day.

THANKSGIVING AT MIDNIGHT IN THE EMERGENCY VET CLINIC

Nobody wants to say
That was the Thanksgiving he died.
We reach

for dry hands 'round
thick tables with leaves
so barely used they're like a slice
of wayward rye lost
in buttermilk. We don't want

to thumb August
magazines slick with strangers'
sweat. Chew through cardboard
cookies while fast toenail
clips and *good girls* whisper
like prayers through too-thin doors.
For an hour

we listened to a woman wail
and keen. Her sobs rocked through membranes,
tore through pericardium. *I wanted*
to see him. Say goodbye. Tell him
it's okay, how much I'll always, always
love him. All the clichés
that don't hurt 'til they're real.
That Thanksgiving

I made a deal—a spooned-out hole
of my atrium, a space to cradle
her pain as my own. Traded my heart
for time. When our
towel-wrapped miracle returned,
eyes kitten black with sticky
forgiveness, I wiped my lashes
and held my breath. Grateful
for a heartbeat, a shot of fur
into the crate, god-bargained thankful
for another holiday we won't remember.

WHEN TO STAY

They say I don't know when to leave, I say
they don't know
when to stay. What good comes
after the bars shut down, past the window of
these shoes could go all night? Knowing when
to stay is what brought me to you.
Knowing how to stay shot us
through the affairs, the culture battles,
the year I ran away to another land with another man
and yet you played stowaway
in my organs. When you know
when to stay, how to close down
the party and watch the lights come on,

you see everything. The way the floors
are caked in syrup and the booths
are worn to threads. How the dancers
wear their stretch marks and the barbacks'
fingernails are chewed. We stayed through

the last song, the final bathroom checks,
when the last dish was scraped of tots
and plopped into the machine—through the ugly
and into the empty morning streets
where New and Hope trudge soft
and amble on bare feet into the next.

GLUTTONY

The cherries, the birds
got them all, gobbled them up—
spit down the pits
for the lawnmower to chew through.
I was five, and the blank fields
went on for acres. Each spring
the blossoms birthed, the fruits
got heavy and the birds
got fat, feasted like winged gods.

ASHIATSU IN THE BEDROOM

How much do you weigh? Come,
walk on my back. You treat me like a child,
a Thai prostitute, Buddhist monk,
all the above—and I love it,

the sense of precariousness, one slip and I fall
like a delicate vase, already cracked and chipped
with age and mistakes but for now radiating
pure lightness, my white feet pressing firm and lovely
into the creamed brown hide of your back.
One pound less and I'd vanish,
one pound more and you'd crumble.
My worth is weighed in ounces, your wants

by the ton.

MAE UN TANG IN YOGA PANTS

I see the men who look at me, the young ones,
the white ones, the boys whose muscles
have barely swollen past puberty. They're the ones
who were sharpened like knives to think
me beautiful. They whistle from their cars, demand,
Show me your tits! as they stoop in bus stops. I tell them,
You could be my child, as I glide by, all tiny
thighs and wasp's waist that seems snappable
as an apple core in their grabbing, greedy hands.
They look at me

like the Koreans do at fish stews—gluttonous
for the fragile bones poking out dangerously
from pale flesh. They see me as something fit
for their mouths, enjoyed in gulps
and forgotten the moment it's swallowed.
I'm not beautiful, not to them—

not in their barbarous parts, the inky spots

pushed down like bad dreams. I'm what they're told

is desirable, what they're supposed to like—

a human substitute for wooden hangers. This,

it isn't beauty. It's a stench that pulses outward

into the streets, intoxicating in the severity

and shockingly eye-catching in the rot.

PICKLE BACKS

When a widower asks
to buy you a shot and your stools
are pushed tight
together against the bar,
say yes as he fingers
a wedding ring. You ever
had a pickle back? and you nod
because grief gives you freedom
to demand whatever you like.
The bourbon licked fever
past the fossa while the brine
bit back, but I thought
this sacrifice kinder than a fuck
on foreign sheets where repentance
tongues fire past the fornix
as the bitterness gnaws deep.

DESPAIR-ITY

I'm embarrassed to say where I came from.
That I didn't always know
how to order a martini, eat roe
from my fist. I've gotten pretty damned
good at it. Faking it, playing make believe,
dress up and pretend. For that,
I practiced. Still,

what if someone finds out? My defenses
crouch close to boiling over, hungry
to pounce—claw at those probing faces.
Like when I get laughed at for my bad
French accent. Called out when I don't know
the difference between tray and recessed
ceilings or what the hell wainscoting
may be. The quiet one, the weird one,
the one who's always watching. Hell,

yes I'm always watching. Observing

like a solid method actor. How else
am I supposed to know what to say?
How to hold a snifter or which cheek
 to kiss first? You should know,
it's exhausting. Terrifying. Smothering
and so overbearingly lonely

way, way over here.

CRAFTS WITH BLUNT EDGES

I cut you out, like those crooked paper dolls
or the gingerbread house walls
that never stuck no matter
how much icing or gobs of gum drops I used.
 I slashed you away like all the others—
the ones I walked away from brisk
with a clip, no lingering
kisses or wondered what-ifs. It's always
been easy to leave, to turn my back
and trust that I alone
am enough to lift myself above the wreckage.

GENETICALLY ISOLATED SINCE THE ICE AGE

I starved myself down the wrong way,
not with a wailing stomach and day-long naps,
but with the kind of hunger you reserve for pure hatred
(or fear)
I was an animal
gutting turkeys, chewing through a cow's gristle
pushing through bags of raw vegetables and passing
on all offers of sweet whiskey, the good bread puddings
and perfect gin martinis with perfect slices of ice
that had kept me warm and fat
bundled in thick layers of subcutaneous blubber
for all those lonely years
I hadn't sprung up like a flower
and I didn't wither like one either.
Not me, for me
it was the failing predator's way,
a flailing Kodiak bear dragging a rusted
trap in my wake so you can all see where I've been

until the starvation caught me

tackled me to the earth and I breathed in the musk

of where we're all going

the embrace turning more tender

as the weight sloughed off until all that's left

is a solid block of sharp bones wrapped tight

in a fancy pantsuit of new muscle so young

and so shiny

and so utterly unlike who I am

or who I thought I was,

I don't know how to wear it right

and it's just so painfully

heartbreakingly obvious

I'm playing dress-up in a closet I don't belong

EMERGENCY PREPAREDNESS

I've learned to roll through your storms
like a Kansan figures out real quick

bathtubs usually stay put in a twister.
For you I hung on

to the rusted pipes,
the gurgling sounds, the cool slickness
of the underbelly. Our years showed me
to wait out the quiet, bear down hard
and not scramble to drown the silence
just because.

I memorized your moods—
unspoken languages are the easiest,
most dangerous to unravel. Now,
I realize when you chop up my pet names
coarse and rough into senseless Hindi
you're happy, ripping at the seams with smiles

and spilling over with touches. When you're hungry,
your skin needs a drink first, lapping up lukewarm
shower rain and Dove soap. And when you won't speak,
I can't make you. I shouldn't even try. I know
how to weather the seasons, how to not get soaked
in the storms and where my secret
umbrellas of strength are kept, bundled tight
and ready to burst open with the slightest push.

MEN

There was the boy who asked *How*
do I know it's mine? before I had the carelessness
sucked out. The one I left on impulse
after seven nothing years—who,
when I asked years later why
he didn't fight for me, said *I realized*
you weren't worth fighting for. Remember

the one who looked so damned good
at the bar in that across the room second—
the alcoholic I traded cries with, crumpled
in his medical scrubs? Then there was the man

whose dreadlocks whipped my arms raw, lucked
in with a visa lottery who fed me sips of rum
on our first date. His accent was lovely, heady
and congealed but still,

he wasn't you. You usurped them all,

needled deep into my meat, the organs,

into the weight of my bones,

the everything of all I had to give.

JUAN G.

For a year he cut the lawn, and I never
knew his last name. I had to ask

the neighbor in the yellow
house after he vanished, her roses
dormant witnesses in the dark. When I'd tried
in terrible Spanish to explain where to plant the lavender,
my *macete* stumbled out *machete*
and he'd laughed behind black cheap
glasses, said, *Police, bad, they don't
like it.* Words fall out clumsy, twisted,
and his surname—
we only cared when he'd gone. Then,

it was knocks on doors, furtive
asks in the night. For a week I watched
the online detainee locator site,
made calls that never came back.
The neighbor patrolled his church, carried

back stories of an avocado orchard
outside Tancítaro, unravelling
acres of drug cartels with *fuerte*-slick lips
where his father-in-law was murdered
last month. We don't know to hope

that ICE ripened him out or if he turned scared
and went south. Children hunkered
in cabs with grass clippings, his wife
watching the exit signs fall
to one. *Who knows?* the neighbor
said, her white teeth shining. *Maybe one day
he'll show up with a truck of avocados*

and his cataracts scraped clean.

THE ROSE

I heard my sister sing
before I knew her, years
before we met. Picking through old
cassettes in the front room, the scent
of mold and sweat, my father's beautiful
handwriting soared like wings
across yellowed masking tape. I didn't know
an Angela, but I knew her voice like my own.
Smoky and anxiously wild. For three hours I listened
to her urge "The Rose" into untamed
blossom. My mother stumbled
upon me in tears, destroyed the tape
and slapped my head. I'd be grown
before I held her, heard
her sing again. Now, gone, my memory
replays her voice in my mind, grainy
and clicking like tired tapes do.

"EATING LIKE A BIRD, IT'S REALLY A FALSITY"

—Norman Bates

You don't just decide to start eating again, it happens
slow, a groggy crawl and stumble out of a dream.
I didn't choose to starve myself, I didn't choose to stop.
It was a cycle, my own metamorphosis
full of Kafka leanings and sopping new wings.

Built up like an orgasm, I can't tell you
the foreplay, the spots touched that got me there,
the details of the teasing
or the fetishes reveled in (that's sacred)
but I can tell you this—I woke up
in Washington Park, stomping the trails behind the zoo.
Maybe it was the humbling houses of the West Hills,
or the reservoirs spreading like spilt champagne
at my feet, but on that day

I woke with a start. Past the rose test garden poached
with pale tourists, past the fountain where droplets
sound like church bells, I climbed to the playground
at the top of the hill,
slipped onto a swing and learned
all over again
how easy it is to fly. My god, it's a lovely thing to face
your fragility and still take flight. But birds,
"birds really eat a tremendous lot," so give me
the fat ones, the thick ones, the ones deep,
fill me with their earthiness until I choke from the grit,
desperate for air, neck arching and jaw flexing,
bones slight and delicate as a song.

NAMESAKES

My mother named me after her
father she hated. Like buying Papo's notice
with a fat grandchild would make up
for anything.

My mother
named me after famous cowboys
then went and married an NDN
herself. Meanwhile her own
mother said *No*
darker. My mom named me
the second most popular girls
name in 1981 because firsts
were for good girls without
panic. My middle
name was the same as a boy
in sixth grade with greasy
nails and dirty hair so I
said it was short for Colette.

My mother was a surprise
fifteen years too late. In the hospital,
her father said, *She ain't much
to look at, is she?* and asked
the nurse to name her. The little Mexican
girl chose Rita after her own
child and nobody not nowhere ever
could say a pearl was an ugly thing.

My mother named me
for a man she despised well
after his girth had gone
to skeleton and the coffin flies
went still—but still,
I thought a namesake
should mean something
good and holy like clean
slates, buried shames and starting overs.

MORNING PASTRIES

You smell like bread in the mornings, something
I want to curl into. Rising yeast and cardamom
notes. It's in the early hours when you're sweetest,
unable to open both eyes and black ribbons of hair
break free from yesterday's oil. Your heat bakes
into the blankets like an oven—that's why
I come back after my tea, after the lemon squeezes,
after the first writings pour from my fingertips.
In tangled sheets and waves of duvets
I ride the surf into the morning sun with you,
tucked safe as a child in your arms.

CHRISTMAS CHAI

That Christmas I gave you an aphotic
steel teapot and you taught me
how to make chai.
I filled the gaping vessel's mouth with tap water
while you peeled slices of unwashed
ginger root. Cardamom pods, cracked
with your crooked teeth
and pried open with fingernails, tossed
helpless in the boil. Milk
comes last,
an opaque white stream
soothing dark spiced water.

The sweetness we could never agree on.

My slow honey, your raw
sugar. That Christmas you gave me words wrapped
in a lilting accent and I taught you
how to say I love you.

I opened my mouth to take you in
while you peeled away clothes from the night
before to spoon,
together, on the mattress.
You bit my shoulder, red fissures from teeth
while I pulled your frenzied hair. Lost together
in the cheap red sheets,
I never came last.
And the sweetness
we could never agree on.

LOVELY IN THE STRANGE

The words in your head
roll in an alien language, all *Bh* and *Kh*
aspirations my tongue refuses to contort
into creation like some bizarre circus of the mouth.
Your dreams tangle like tipsy lovers in culture, place
I'll never understand, worlds away
from my own. I don't want to know you,
not every crevice,
not every space. Let the others breed
contempt, our crashes are made up
of a perfect Venn diagram, rich
in mystery and lovely in the strange.

LOVE YOU MORE

I sent you a keychain stamped *love*
you more from my crumbling
Costa Rican hacienda. You were turning thirty
and we had years of regrets
stitched and scarred
up and down our arms like teenagers
in the grip of delusion, tired dogs
after the fights. I waited

until you caught
up with me to say
I was coming back,
my muscles tensed, fat
scars ropy thick, ready for a blossoming
explosion black as your eyes
swimming beneath heavy
brow and deafening
as your lips wrapped
like a vise around my name.

SATYAVACHAN

Say something in Gujarati and I see you
as you were years ago, in the bars
next to gargantuan women, faded flowers
suckling your youth, moving quick as hummingbirds
flashing crow's feet with a deftness
that blurred their age. Feed me by hand
like you used to, change my water for yours,
the one ringing with ice
and tell me you love me
even throughout all the changes,
after all these years.

My father told me, *Be careful,*
you have that wandering way.

Just like him, whom I see in your slowness
to laugh, the oil slicks of your eyes. I chose
you, I choose
an incredible life.

HOW DYING IS DONE

They always tell you it's like a cancer, horse piss
spearing thick as butter into perfect alabaster,
but it's not like that at all.
When the black sickness began to crawl
up my arm, claws
dug in deep, inching up forearms
wrapped tight in veins,
the paramedics and nurses and doctors were right,
It did look like cancer--but cancer,
it has more modesty
or shame than that. I watched it spread,
arching and keening like a crazed lover
while the doctors filed in, pudgy, tired penguins
telling me time and again
We don't know what this is, but this, this
is how dying is done.

We'll cut off the arm
to save the head and heart.

I'd heard that before,

year after knife twisting year,

but an amputation doesn't stop It.

Cuts aren't clean,

no matter who's wielding the scalpel.

God, I waited for the clichés, for the lights

or the montage or the regrets

to pour in as the monsoon,

but that's not how dying is done.

You keep on wanting

what your heart's been suffocating,

bearing down underneath blood and muscle, but still

It refuses to drown, what your head

turns away from, holding up ridiculous

mobiles and distractions that even a child

wouldn't fall for. You.

You were what I wanted

when the darkness set in, so furious and real

that It refused to stay buried like a guilt-soaked

secret. We'd grown into something so much heavier,

something of such Botero grandiosity,

that not even a vehicle as strong as my body
could keep it quiet or stop it from bursting into blossom.

PILOT'S LOG: DAY 23

When I was learning to fly, he killed
the engine. Said, *You don't need power to stay
here*. And he was right,
but the silence,
the silence is maddening.
In the quiet your heart blunders
like a drunk against ear drums. Buttons
press aching into pelvis, you notice
how much bigger your thighs
are than his. This

is so amazingly stupid, and radio
static is syrup-
thick while tiny homes below
beg like scared children for you
to come crashing back down.

GENETICS

My mother told me I was a sociopath
because You don't like touching, unable
to imagine it was her musky skin,
dust-dry lips that made me shrink.
She'd smack my head and demand
kisses on lips—even in Kindergarten
I had a fathoming
of what incest was. Burned something
fierce when I spiraled my father's
oiled hair into two spikes
and said, *I'm making you
horny.* How does a child know
such things, isn't shame
learned or is it something seedy
and genetic? Like my mandibular
tori, bone growths
filling my mouth like cement, but still

unable to stop the fattening

and the disgraces falling out.

HOW I LIKE MY WOMEN

I like my women slight and frail, bones
hollowly light, ribcages pressed
like prison bars against the skin.
I love the women with stomachs caved in,
divots carved like ice cream scoops
below breasts begging to melt. It's the women
with the lips like readied blisters, skin sautéed
in good genes and creams
that remind me how exquisite we are
and of all I'll never be.

ROOM ENOUGH

You once told me I'd never be
the most beautiful woman in the room,
so what nakedness of my flaws were pancaked opaque
enough to trick you so close? So what
if I'm always the palest in the crowd, my lips hike
above the gum line when I laugh or if tired
flanks my eyes like a bustle? Maybe,

for you,

I'm the last one here in this echo chamber. The others
left, halted out of their youth in a daze, got comfortable
in wilting skin, found solace in fat and pants
with too much give. Every woman wants
a room of her own, one with a view—a place
where the secrets roam free and the knocks
come as soft flurries at the thick door like children
spilling over with cheap Halloween sugar
and rolled like caterpillars into fall apart costumes.

LATTES AND LABIAPLASTY

How good are you at unpacking? Real
damn good and fast—I beat everyone at
emptying the suitcase after vacation.
No, I mean your feelings, your emotions. Oh, real
fucking good. I slam those things into drawers
and closets so quick you can't be certain,
not totally, that was a stain you saw
on the sleeve. All these new words
are so careful, the phrases so contrived. Nobody
wants to be all woman, and here I am
apologizing for not envying his cock
or whipping out credit cards
for labiaplasty. On the inside,
I picture a half-man goat sucking
a flute when I say I'm pan-sexual,
such a ridiculous word for lust
without limits. Who cares
who I bed or what my testosterone
levels are today? Unpack this, dismantle

that, something about patriarchy
and pretend women have zero privileges.
How's this for privilege: I pass
as white and all the freedom
that carries, will never be falsely
accused of rape, and when I wear high heels
I trade perceived weakness for doors held
open and comped lattes with foam
like waning orgasms. We set the price,
finger the terms and choose by the day
the space we spoon from this world.

THE TEMPORARY NATURE OF BEING

Bedded down in the woods,
the houses rest on stilts, dangling like sleeping
children on top bunks. We tiptoe like gluttons
across the Cascadia faults,
as if the sweets stuffed in cupboards
and ice cream cradled in freezers are fair
trade for our lives. The experts call us
woefully unprepared as we bow tangled
heads over sugary cereal, the morning
news unable to shock. Tsunamis overseas,
floods on the east coast—we're so sure
nothing can touch us here, not in the Wild
West, never where gold rushes raged
or Martinis were brought to life. Forest hugs
me close, the occasional sharp thorny fingernails
tracing taut calves or hoggish spider webs
licking my face.
One day, soon, it will all come crashing down:

The West Hills homes indie bands made famous,
the teetering decks like behemoths,
dumb and feeble scarecrows in the sky.

KITCHEN VOLCANOES

On the slabs we pull apart turkey carcasses,
you feed me diced paneer, wet and chilled,
in pinched fingers.
It's where you make your evening mess, where I wipe
up your powders and crumbs, and where the lassi erupts
from our broken blender and bleeds
into the cracks and pores. Granite is an untamed thing—
volcanic, unpredictable, a force of a siren.
Deep in the magma chambers, melted rock oozes.
Sometimes the vile is spewed out in a bulimic fashion,
sometimes, it waits for hundreds of thousands of years.
Rocks cool slowly like forgotten indiscretions.
Patience makes the heat forget, the boiling subside.
In the end, stoicism can erode a mountain, a volcano,
even you.

Lifetimes later,
granite rises to the earth's surface, scrubbed clean

and stone cold to strangers, children, everyone but us.
We make countertops from it, slice our dinners,
spill our drinks and break the glasses.

TO BREAK FAST

Life crept back into me like a child slipping
into the Big Bed in the middle of the night. Slowly,
silently, so as not to disturb
the sleeping giants within. I was light
in a way starvation never allowed,
lucid, the bony fingers of dangerous dreams slipping
off my shrunken arms. Just as nightmares
aren't welcome when a girl spoons close
to her mother's sleeping body, as they're scared
into submission by her father's monstrous snores,
my desire to vanish lifted like a morning stretch,
dissipating with a yawn at the pink, dawning light.

RECIPE FOR MOONG DAAL

Look at me like you did
the first time you made me moong daal,
my Otis Redding and Eartha Kitt
uncertain in the tiny, dirty kitchen
and you, oiled black ringlets
falling like madmen on your brow.
Press me hard against the counter,
knead your hands
into my waist, trace your fingers
over hip bones,
invade my mouth with yours
between the squealing whistles
of the pressure cooker.
Oil heating in the saucepan, dusted
with cumin seeds,
watch them struggle til they're the same
soft brown as your hairless arms
pulling me close, between the stove
and you. We tear dried red

chilies into the pan, adding the spice.
Dice slick green peppers
on a makeshift cutting board, thick
fingers deftly working the small,
fragile slivers with the same certainty
they handle me. Grate in ginger root
with rhythmic practice, add the curry leaves.
Onions and turmeric are next
as I lean against the refrigerator,
breathing you in, the scent of your sweat
with the bite of red onions.
Grab me tight, taste my neck
while the turmeric spreads golden
in the hiss. A pinch of asafoetida,
all the pan holds poured into the cooker
and for ten minutes you deconstruct
me, long ginger-scented fingers
stained yellow brushing my lips,
black onion-teary eyes searching
and the blues
crying like forgotten children.

THE THINGS I DO FOR YOU

The things I do for you
are without thinking,
no scores kept or favors stacked.
It's in the simplicity, the ease
that I know now—as I always have—
that loving you is natural, as much
a part of me as my crooked eyebrows.
That's why

I give you the good pieces
of bread, the thickest morsels
torn from cookies, the water
with the least ice (I know
how you hate the cold.)

THE SWEET BELOW THE BITTER

I still want you to make me orange juice, to squeeze,
press and twist the rinds in your pillowy palms,
to make room in the freezer
because you know that's how I like it,
enceinte with pulp and buried in a layer of ice
I can crack as easily as your heart. I still listen
to the rhythm every night, the cycle of blood
and all the little things inside you
I'll never know completely—even if I wanted to, even
if I wasn't terrified of the fallout. Let me taste
the carpel, the sweet after the albedo bitter
and I'll drink it down not caring
of the trails like slugs left behind.

WHAT I FOUND IN THE SWAMP

It was the bayous that showed us where we'd been,
in that bastard salt freshwater stewing
with alligators and swamp piss. Miles from New
Orleans, I snaked my arm through yours while spray
from the airboat slapped my face, not nearly as hard
as your snapping words of the past three years
had managed. Killing
the engine and docked beneath a haggard
cypress tree, roots sprouting and sucking
at air through the marsh, I cradled
a fingerling in frozen hands. Its belly
hung heavy in my palm, trusting stupidly
that I wouldn't crush it for sport, and with only
our thin skins between us, I felt not
even a whisper of heartbeat.

SAVING ROOM

A dessert too sweet? That's nonsense
even as a child I never believed.
Give me the corner piece, buttercream
piled high in shells and roses,
Corneli lace by the foot and sotas for days.

I'd scoop out the cake, an unnecessary social obligation
like dinner before your mouth on mine,
whiskey before shirts on floors,
and feast on sheer frosting, grains crashing against
my teeth rough as the tide—this

is still how I like it, creamed nipples
and syrup on collarbones, rivering down,
down, into the devil's food of our bodies moist
and molten in a way fondant artists and bakery slaves
never imagined pulling from the heat.

SOMETHING SWEET

Do you want something sweet?
Your toddler came at me like a bacchanal,
mouth open with desire. Imagine
being that trusting, certain
that what was placed on your tongue would please,
the sugar grains scrubbing down your palate,
the ghee melting like perfection down your throat.

Kadri didn't know I called the besan ladoo *sandballs*,
that they required the perfect mix of chickpea
and kadalai maavu, that the elachi was the secret
or that you had to sieve the flour just right. All he knew

was that *sweet* was something good, that hands
were made for his pleasures. Imagine
being that naïve, the beauty in opening your mouth.

TABLE D'HOTE

Everything would be easier had I never found you,
but who wants a simple life? Give me the hard stuff,
the twists that leave us lurching and introversions
that make hearts gush. I see the settling
all around me—comforts others cling
to like pilled blankets. I watch their waists
expand, habits stick like sloshed batter
on hot stovetops. And it's devastating,
that slow shuffle back to the earth. Their heads
tuck down into heavy, invisible feedbags
as the fattening season drones on, but we,
we've carried on. The two of us,
we carry on.

EATING

A man makes love the way he eats, you
always devoured the daal
like a starving animal, thick fingers
yellowed with turmeric pinching
the steaming naan, over-ripened
lips slick with the juices of burst
lentils. Afterward, you did the same
to me, tearing at my flesh, hungry
and never sated. For years
I watched you suck and lap
up everything laid before you
and I realized I would never be
enough to satisfy the craving
that purrs within.

STILL

Yes, I love you still
something stupid (please
stop asking). I can't say why,
there aren't new epiphanies
each day. It's the same
keeping on reasons as always—straight
from the beginning.
You don't remember all the everythings
that drew me close. The
You wear a wicked grins and hand
feedings on makeshift tables.
Those are the whys and they build,
stack upon one another like scaffolding,
like us, like how we knew,
like stubborn children We would rise.

DRAG ME THROUGH THE MESS

Love stories aren't tidy and wrapped up in ribbons—
at least not ours
and that's how I like it. Drag me

through the mess, the neuroses pressed into your brain
by the hands that wove your childhood jalebi
and tell me something nice
that makes me feel pretty, something

crafted with nuances and peppered
with subtleties that neither of us fully believe,
but the lies so sweet and drenched in syrupy half-truths

we can't help but binge on the gluttony,
engorging ourselves on each other.

GOOD MEDICINE

Today I wrote my fiftieth poem and it
was about you. Funny how that works,
how our histories sneak up on us
like boogeymen to children's dreams.
I never wanted to be a doctor's
wife—it's a title bestowed upon the damned
like a king knighting a warrior
before sending him to glory-full death. I want
to make my own name, watch it grow
wild as a sea monkey with my words, not suffocate
with a stiffening smile beneath yours.
You saved my life long before your white
coats grew long to brush those swollen thighs,
because you—you let me go.

THE PROTAGONIST

You got your own book, this
is our love story, pages
brimming with remembers.
The close calls, reversed regrets,
proud colors bleeding out
from the Nehalem days like stiffening pink
peonies. I can't give you much.

My voice sticks in my teeth like chikki.
But I can give you this—

The best of *back whens*,
the worst hours wrapped tight for storage
and me

draped in letters and adorned in poetry.

ACKNOWLEDGEMENTS

Thank you to the Women's International Study Center (WISC); the Acequia Madre House in Santa Fe, NM is where many of these poems were polished. Thank you to the Potlatch Fund for providing incredible support in bringing this collection to life. A big thank you to the publisher, Unsolicited Press, for believing in this "Mess" and nourishing it into the best version of itself. Poetry is never realized alone—I am fortunate to have a bountiful network bustling behind the curtains.

ABOUT THE AUTHOR

Jessica (Tyner) Mehta is a Cherokee poet, novelist, and storyteller. She's the author of ten books including the forthcoming *Savagery* (poetry) and *You Look Something* (literary fiction). She's also the author of the poetry collections *Constellations of My Body*, *Secret-Telling Bones*, *Orygun*, *What Makes an Always*, and *The Last Exotic Petting Zoo* as well as the novel *The Wrong Kind of Indian*. She's been awarded the Barbara Deming Memorial Fund Prize in Poetry, the Potlatch Award for Native Artists, and numerous poet-in-residencies posts around the world including Hosking Houses Trust with an appointment at The Shakespeare Birthplace Trust in Stratford-Upon-Avon, England, and Paris Lit Up in France. Jessica is a poetry editor for Bending Genres Magazine and founder of the Get it Ohm! karma yoga movement. Visit Jessica's author site at www.jessicamehta.com